Shared THOUGHTS

ENGAGING IN LIFE

*Father Wayne
Blessings!
Angela Charles
July 16, 2017*

Angela Charles

Copyright © 2017 by Angela Charles.

Library of Congress Control Number: 2017905166
ISBN: Hardcover 978-1-5434-1347-2
Softcover 978-1-5434-1346-5
eBook 978-1-5434-1345-8

All rights reserved. No part of this book may be reproduced or transmitted in any form or by any means, electronic or mechanical, including photocopying, recording, or by any information storage and retrieval system, without permission in writing from the copyright owner.

Any people depicted in stock imagery provided by Thinkstock are models, and such images are being used for illustrative purposes only.
Certain stock imagery © Thinkstock.

Print information available on the last page.

Rev. date: 04/12/2017

To order additional copies of this book, contact:
Xlibris
1-888-795-4274
www.Xlibris.com
Orders@Xlibris.com
759132

Acknowledgements

Before all else, I thank God for his wisdom and endless love.

My profound gratitude to my biggest cheerleader and light of my life, Tony, for his suggestions and constant encouragement. This book would not be written without him.

My thanks and appreciation to my review team – Raelene Bruney, Frances Delsol, Dorrette Joseph, Juliet Cole – for support and helpful advice.

A thank you to family and friends, who in one way or another, shared their support.

Thanks to you, the reader, for your appreciation and to the publishers for making the book a reality.

Shared
THOUGHTS

Not in my Time, Lord, but in Your Time

I prayed for someone to love me,
You answered, Lord, in your time.
I prayed for someone I could love,
You answered, Lord, in your time.
I prayed for joy and happiness,
You answered, Lord, in your time.
Our future is God centered,
Not self-centered.
Our love will be free and everlasting,
Our union divinely timed.
Our joy and happiness will be boundless.

You, Lord, are the source.
We give you our struggles,
fears, faults, and frustrations.
We give you thanks.
We are grateful, Lord.
We know everything is in your time, Lord,
Not our time, Lord, but Yours.
Your plan, Lord, Your timing.

Love

(Not Romantic Love)

A feeling like no other
different
a range of emotions
heartbreak and sorrow
joy, wonder, happiness
an experience
life.

Love
like the rising sun
slowly emerging
rising higher and higher
with each passing moment
bright
bringing light to everything it touches
wrapping all in its warmth.

There are times
when the clouds obscure the sun
sun setting
dark, rainy days
heartbreaking
love.

Love
like a bud opening
opening to the world
a flower of beauty
exposed
a wonder
magical.

Like the many hues of a rainbow
like numerous flowers
there are all types of love
parental love
unconditional love
romantic love
love of country
emotional
heartfelt
magical
love.

Love
giving of itself
receiving happiness
receiving joy
love.

First Meeting

Excitement
anxious
a million scenarios
liking each one
acting out each one.

Heart beating
blood pumping
sweating.
Time getting closer for
the first eye contact,
the first touch,
the first impression.
Will it be
joy or sadness,
Smiles or grimace
Hope or disappointment?

At last—the meeting.
time is suspended
world shrinks.
One-on-one,
face-to-face
the first look
the first touch.
Finally
heart rate slows
the weight lifts
the sun is shining
the world is alive
excitement
exhilaration
smiles
joyful hope
the first meeting.

Longing for You

Morning comes
I turn over
Where are you?
Longing, longing for you.

Missing the little things,
the big things,
your voice,
your laughter.
Joy and happiness
now emptiness
no one else
only you to hold, to love
warmth and contentment.
Longing, longing for you.

Longing
for days that are endless
time of no consequence
sun shining on raining days
my answered prayer
closeness and peace.

Darkness
I close my eyes.
You are my light, my love
longing, longing for you.

Positions

You and I
intimate moments
the love dance
musical creations.

One step, two steps
this position, that position
ever changing
the music
the dance.

We in our rhythm
time stops
thoughts suspended
passion rising
position changing
the music
changing
flying
dance escalating
ecstasy rising
freedom
release
love.

I Love You

I smile
your voice
on the phone, face-to-face
intimate
joy and happiness
my world is alive.

I love you
your kisses
soft, gentle
giving, receiving.

Your touch
electrifying
stirring
reaching deep
rendering me
mindless.

I am thankful for you
you make me feel
safe
protected
cherished
loved.

My one, my only
my heart
my valentine
take my hand
together
our love
forever
I love you.

Yellow Flowers

It's hard
the waiting
you picked yellow flowers
patience.

You talk.
we talk.
I wait.
patience
yellow flowers.

We laugh
we connect
patience
yellow flowers
waiting.

Loving,
waiting
yellow flowers
patience.

The Breakup

A text
impersonal
emotionless
a few words
it's not you
no explanation
no future contact
the breakup.

Today's reality
using technology to hide
faceless cowards
easier
easier to breakup.

Expectations
dinner, dancing, a ring
instead
incoming text
breaking up.

Bewilderment
confusion
anger
tears
the breakup.

Questions
what did I miss?
what did I do?
where did I go wrong?
it was not you.
impersonal text
faceless breakup.

Sadness and heartbreak
name-calling
no closure
Tweeting
Instagram
The breakup.

Written for all mothers—not just for those who gave birth

Manman (Mother)

You gave birth to me
you are my new mammy.
you are my other mother.
you adopted me.
ou sé tout manman
you are all mothers.

Keeper of my heart
enduring sleepless nights
endless crying
cradling me
not complaining
simply loving me.

Manman moi
I held your hand.
I listened to you.
I loved you even when I no longer held your hand,
even when I gave you attitude,
even when I caused you anguish, grief, and sadness.

My mother
thank you
for taking me through life's stages
and loving me despite my complaints
failures and shortcomings.

I honor you today and every day.
my own earthly angel
my conscience
the voice in my head
manman moi
I love you.

I pray that
Bondyé bèni ou
God bless you,
provide for you,
and keep you in his loving care.
manman moi
my mother.

NOTE
The Kwéyòl (Creole) words in italics are
followed by their English translations.
Although English is the official language of Dominica
(The Commonwealth of Dominica), the people sing,
speak, and write Kwéyòl, which is a French-based Creole
language. Kwéyòl is a unique patois mixed with Caribe,
French, and African vocabulary and grammatical rules.

Creole was the linguistic term used for languages developed
on the slavery plantations when large numbers of West
Africans were transported to the Caribbean.

My Children

My miracles
meaning of my life
my gifts
I love you dearly
I love you forever
my children.

Your birth changed me
blessings
my responsibility
to mold, guide,
teach and protect.
wonder, amazement, stress.
heavenly.

I am proud of you
my children.
you are your own person
kind and thoughtful,
treating others with respect.
you taught me patience,
unconditional love,
humility.

My children
follow your heart
live your dreams
spread your wings.
the world is waiting
I trust your decisions
I support you on your journey
love you dearly
love you forever.

We Are Women

We have roared.
we have protested.
crying out,
shouting.
did you hear us?
did you listen?
we are women.

Burdened
no pay, meager pay
housewife, mother
beaten, molested
pain, rape.
did you turn your back
because we are women?

We continue to roar
stronger, harder, louder
crying out for equality
at home,
at work,
in the community,
in the world
hear us
hear us women.

We give birth to future leaders
we mold young minds.
we sacrifice for you.
we suffer
we endure.

See us
hear us
your wives, mothers, daughters
sisters, aunts, teachers
see us women.
respect and fairness.

We believe in possibilities
we overcome challenges
we have hope
we know our strengths,
our gifts.
no limits
no boundaries
we are amazing.
we are women.

My Sisters

Colorful,
standing proud,
standing tall,
unapologetic
you have a special place for me in your heart.
You defend me.
I am you.
My sister.

Hair
You invented and perfected style
long, short,
straight, curly, kinky,
natural, processed,
braids, locs
not forgetting weaves and wigs
topping it off with the head wrap.

My sisters
different sizes,
different shapes,
mostly curvy
an array of facial features
our proud heritage on display.

The color of your skin
a source of envy
a source of self-shame
a source of pride
light cream to deep mahogany
and every hue in between
colors on an artist's palette
beautiful, unique
but still cause for hatred
my sisters.

We look to history for our sheroes and mentors
mothers—not giving in, not giving up
believing in a dream
activists, writers, poets, entrepreneurs, professionals
dreams can come true.
former First Lady Michelle Obama
anything is possible
borne from hardship and poverty
borne from love and determination
we survive
we flourish
we succeed
you lift me up
you are my reflection
My sisters.

Memories of You

We are all older
memories remain
some faded
you are still close
still present.

You are with us as we walk
on paths seen and unforeseen
alone, together
unafraid, hopeful, or
mired in the mud of our own making.

Your leaving was sudden
unexpected
it brought change
the kids, still young
in a boat with no rudder
adrift
still searching
still clinging
needing a safe harbor
slowly changing
no one was immune
you were part of us
we had to go on
some evaluated their lives
made changes, changed dreams
pursued goals, attained goals
health, family
closeness
others were swept along
going with the flow
no growth
no change.

We remember you
a thought away
our lives forever
changed on that day
now
share our journey
we will always be
together.

Breathe

Life
my daughter, my sons
grandchildren
teenagers and newborn
smile
breathe
in and out.

Sunshine
hope and promise
brothers and sisters
family
one breath, two breaths.

Home and hearth
warmth, friends
love and prayers
breathe life.

Joy
memories
breathe, breathe
breathe life.

Life

Celebrate
new beginnings
family
birth
successes
feast joyfully
feast fully
celebrate life.

Rejoice
life's many blessings
thankful
for the gift of health
give love
receive love
happiness
laughter
see the light
lift up another
life.

Reflect
learn from the past
learn from mistakes
go within
forgive
embrace change
make a better life.

Life
rejoicing and celebrating
unpredictable
days, months, years
in despair and turmoil.
prayer and faith
belief
love and hope
you are not alone
life.

The Journey

The egg hatches.
The bird struggles.
It staggers
Rights itself, looks.
A new world
Places to soar.
Things to do.

So many like me.
My parents know best
My teachers continue the work
I will emulate
I will listen
I will learn
My language
My community.

My wings are strong
Strong enough to soar
New lands to conquer.
Listen and Learn.
Teach and support.
Battered and bruised
I grow strong.

I remember
My parents' love
My parents' words
Your support.

I will continue my work
To love you
To love my community
To love my country
Battered and bruised
I will continue to soar
I am strong
I will shelter you
The journey continues.

Let Go and Release

We hold on tight
to pain, burdens, anger, grief
keeping them close.
unable to let go
keeping us stuck
unable to release.

Every burden unique
every anger and guilt personal
no one knows or
understands your grief
my fault, your fault, their fault.
the blame game
blaming God.
cannot let go
cannot forgive
cannot forget.
not letting go.

Know what to release
what to let go.
forgive to be happy
forgive to move on and grow
release and change
change thoughts
look to change
believe.

Release slowly
a life change
burdens lifted
grief shared, understood
anger dissipated
pain lessened
guilt released.

Release with no help
release with help from a friend or family
let it go with professional help
just let it go
for self
for family
release and live fully
live happier
live healthier.

Break Down the Walls

The walls are going up
walls of racism and discrimination
fueled by ignorance, intolerance
and narrow-mindedness
breeding hatred and bigotry
keeping people divided
suspicious, angry
break down the wall
know and respect your neighbor
form friendships
be tolerant.

Fear builds its own wall
paralyzing
casting doubt
becoming a victim
unable to change
unable to grow
break down the wall
change expectations
believe in yourself
be courageous
be bold.

The wall of unforgiveness
must come down
first, forgive yourself
then, forgive the other party
break down the wall
be willing to forgive
forgive to change, to move on
release the hurt.

Walls go up when
there is hurt, betrayal
and unfaithfulness
trust is lost
love dies
break down the walls
heal the wounds
trust again
open your heart
to love.

The Room Door

The door
opens and closes
stays ajar or wide open
you enter, you leave
the door.

Some say that
a door is a door is a door.
others use it
to teach, to illustrate
to demonstrate.

The door
opens to welcome family and friends
inviting
to let the wind blow through
clearing out the cobwebs
bringing change,
warmth and energy
refreshing.

The door
closed to keep you safe
to keep out the dark
to keep out the cold and the wind
to shut out the world.

We do not know
what happens behind a closed door.
people forget their troubles,
show their true colors
secrets are buried
fears, lies, and violence contained
closed doors.

Close the door on a relationship
open one to new beginnings
close the door on a current job
open one to new opportunities
leave it ajar to return
step through the door
embrace hope
embrace change
the door of life
live.

Blindness

Blindness
brought on by one's own making
first impressions
the look
one too many tattoos
dresses in leather
a biker
facial rings
the color of hair
the color of skin
eye color
limited vision
living in the dark
unable to see the light.

Blindness
to the truth
to rules and regulations
to a way of life
loving sinful habits
loving material things
too much to see the light
break the limitations
step into the light.

Blind from birth
from diseases
loss of vision
physical darkness
living in the light
seeing with eyes of the mind.

Blindness
in its many forms
steeped in darkness
in need of spiritual vision
looking for help to see
looking to the Master of the Universe
seeing the light
living in the light.

Music

Music
surrounding you
caressing you
taking you to another place
relaxing, uplifting
mood changer
a range of emotions.

Sounds from the heart
of love and hope
of oppression, wars, and injustice
of freedom and pain
crying out
reality
sounds from the soul
psalms, hymns
praise and worship
joyful sounds
melodies.

Music
from all corners of the world
cultural
no translation required
made on all types of instruments
DIYs, customized, digital
made from the heart.

Music everywhere
at home, in waiting rooms
at weddings and funerals
in movies, dramas and comedies.

Music to the ears
sounds of the wind
crashing waves
sounds in silence
listen and enjoy
the music.

The Beach

Naked feet
sand through toes
sinking
joyful sensations
sun-kissed bodies
warmth
the beach.

The water
inviting
immense
only room for enjoyment
no thoughts
tranquil
no cares
happiness.

The beach
social hangout
playing in the sand
building sandcastles
buried in the sand
walking, playing
beach volleyball
flying kites
Frisbees.

Quiet and reflective
sunbathing
relaxing
people gazing
watching the sunrise and sunset
walking the dog
thinking of taking a swim
the beach.

A Friend

A friend
listens and hears
gives comfort
weeps in empathy
tells the hard truth
is always available
a friend.

First friends
never forgotten
never far
no matter the distance
shared memories
shared joys
always
a friend.

True friend
like diamonds
unearthed in unexpected places
school, work, travels, next door
becoming like family
becoming family
brother, sister
sharing happiness
sharing woes
friendship.

A friend
support, praise
guidance
a shoulder to lean on
a helping hand
a lifting hand
grateful for
a true friend.

The Smile

A smile
beaming
transforming the face
exercising facial muscles
welcoming
captivating
return smiles
speculation
about the smile.

Behind the smile
joy and happiness
a host of reasons
the job, a promotion
surprises and gifts
a compliment
family gathering
seeing friends
taking pictures
even the weather
smiling.

The smile
hides secrets
no one can see
shortcomings
pain and heartache
despair
desperation
failure
keep smiling.

Smile
for yourself
your health
your feelings
your reasons
smile for others
to forgive
invitation
welcome
friendship
to break the ice
to soften the blow
the smile.

Peace

Elusive
desirable
wanting it
yearning for it
some never finding
peace
infants have peace
no cares, no worries
all is well.

Growing older
life happens
stress at home
on the job, pressures at school
worries
no peace.

Stuff happens
searching for peace
divorce—wanting peace
isolation—looking for peace
diseases manifest when there is no peace
suicide or worse
pressure at boiling point
desperate for peace
lashing out
unable to continue.

Finding peace
life's mission
meditation for some
art and music for others
service
giving of self
finding it in family
finding it in love
always possible
to find some peace
Peace.

Dreams

Dreams
seem unattainable.
left unfulfilled,
ever changing,
interrupted
not participating in life
always wondering
wishing.

Dreams
long buried.
changed directions
new plans
followed other people's dreams
no time for dreams
no motivation
no support
lack of funds
someday.

Someday.
life change
job change
spiritual awakening
bringing hope
stepping up
faith
prayers
believing again
getting support
charting new directions
dreams.

Heart desires
coming alive
taking action
taking control
hopes and dreams
fulfillment.

Loneliness

Darkness
feeling numb
walls closing in
lethargic
no appetite
no motivation
isolation
loneliness.

Alone in a crowd
standing apart
lost
words, music
unheard
no interest
no pleasure
cannot escape
loneliness.

Alone in a marriage
feeling ignored
unappreciated
no communication
no love
together but alone.

Escape
in technology
hide in isolation
delve into books
searching for an out
needing help
needing a friend
loneliness.

Movement

Young children
running
playing
climbing up and down
constant movement
developing young muscles
movement.

Older children
some participating in sports
moving their bodies
others choosing technology
little or no movement
weight issues
health challenges
movement.

Adults
reminders
move it or lose it
movements
get off the couch
go to the gym
exercise at home
run, walk
walk the dog
dance
just move.

Movement
health benefits
alert mind
toned body
looking ageless
relieving stress
movement.

Raindrops

Gloomy day
rain and wind
listening
raindrops against the window
the sound bringing back
memories of younger days.

The sound of raindrops
on the roof
musical
soothing
running between the raindrops
showering with raindrops
snuggling with siblings
drinking hot cocoa tea
innocence
comfort
sweet memories
raindrops.

Raindrops against the window
remembering
innocence and comfort
memories
smiling
Snuggling
sipping hot cocoa
raindrops.

City Lights

So many
colorful
lighting the way
keeping back the dark
feeling safe
city lights.

So bright
forgetting to look up at the stars
missing the moonlight
focusing on
our errands
our travels
on the neon lights
the city lights.

Looking down on
the city at night
memories of Christmas
come rushing back
the lights
the colors
moving car lights
amazing with snow
always gladness
inner peace
a joy to behold
magnificent.

The view from above
spectacular
a cause of wonder
an array of lights
a kaleidoscope
hearts always glad
never tiring of the view
a sea of endless lights
the splendor of
city lights.

Winter

Short days
bundling up against
the cold, snow, and wind
dressing layer upon layer
Winter.

Freezing rain
creating havoc
walking impossible
slipping, sliding, falling
cars uncontrollable
snow tires or not
forgetting the ice scraper
no deicer
shoveling, heavy lifting
salt to the rescue
Winter.

Pristine snow—so clean
picturesque
begging for snow angels
snow days and snowmen
snowball fights
embrace Winter
Winter fun.

Skiers and skateboarders
skates taken out of storage
hockey season
time to ice fish
time for ice wine
hot apple cider tastes so much better.

Winter
runny nose, fever, coughs
aches and flu
chicken soup and medication
sleet and slush
snow squalls, snowstorms, and whiteouts
waiting for Spring
to be repeated.

Rain Showers

The sun is warm
the wind caressing
God is smiling down on me
joy and peace.

Rain clouds appear
the sun disappears
the wind blows
shadows form
no preparation
no time to hesitate
shelter from the trees.

Water drips
clothes soaked
time passes
the rain stops
always, always
the sun comes out
rain showers.

Edwards Brothers Malloy
Ann Arbor MI. USA
April 28, 2017